COCKAPOO TRAINING MANUAL

The Ultimate Essential Practice Guide to an Obedient Trained Cockapoo

CURTIS LITTLE

Copyright@2020

TABLE OF CONTENT

CHAPTER ONE 4
   Introduction: 4
   What is Cockapoo? 4
   History: 5
   Physical characteristics: 7
   Behavior and temperament: 10
CHAPTER TWO 11
   House training: 11
   Potty training: 11
   Rewarding positive behavior: 14
   Crate training: 14
CHAPTER THREE 20
   Training in terms of exercise: 20
   Importance: 20
   Types: 22
   Mental exercise: 25
CHAPTER FOUR 27
   Socializing the cockapoo: 27
   Introducing cockapoo with new people: ...27
   Introducing with other puppies: 29

Conclusion: 31

CHAPTER ONE

Introduction:

Cockapoo is a type of dog which is found in various parts of world. This book will be going to discuss the Cockapoo breed. It will be discussing the adoption and training methods of puppy. For a new owner, the training of a puppy is very critical. It needs a complete guide to make things clear after having a puppy. All training and puppy adoption will be discussed in details in this article.

What is Cockapoo?

The Cockapoos basically a cross between a Cocker Spaniel and a Poodle. As it can be bred from a broad range of parents, it can vary greatly in appearance and size, as can its character traits. A Cockapoo is a dog crossbreed bred from a Cocker Spaniel and a Poodle, most commonly the Miniature Poodle. The Cockapoo was first bred in the United States by

designer dog breeders to produce a healthy companion dog; hybrid vigor is believed to prevent the crossbreed.

The Cockapoo is actually the first of the "designer breeds" (not a purebred dog breed), more than just a hundred years old, dating back to the 1960s. A cute, little dog with the attitude of a huge clown.

History:

Cockapoos, also referred to in some

regions as Cockerpoos, or Spoodles in Australia, originated in the US and have been a popular mixed-breed or hybrid dog since at least the early 1960s and possibly earlier. Although these sturdy little dogs are not recognized as a breed group by the AKC, some dog clubs carefully breed consecutive generations to ultimately establish cockapoos as a recognized breed. Meanwhile, relative to many purebred animals, cockapoos usually have the luxury of a long-life cycle.

The rapidly growing success of cockapoos is no surprise. The Cockapoos have a lot of things going for them. They are exceptionally knowledgeable, agile, vigorous, low-shedding dogs with fur that is fluffy, almost dander- free.

The American Cockapoo Club was founded in 2004; these members don't combine generations back to a Poodle or a Cocker Spaniel and don't breed a Cockapoo. "They still have a show dogs, and their goal is to" see authentic Cockapoos raised with lines which can be mapped back to the originating origins of AKC / CKC Cocker Spaniels and AKC / CKC Poodles.

Breeding philosophies aside, the success of the Cockapoo has not only remained steady, it has evolved over the decades. The Cockapoo, in one shape or another, may be on its way to being something more than a "designer breed" with the help of conscientious breeders and national associations and clubs.

Physical characteristics:

It is normally a small to medium, light-framed breed, weighing between 5 and 10 kg (11-22 lb.), and between 20-30 cm (8-12 in) in height, although the Cockapoo will obviously come in many different sizes. It has a relatively long, soft and fuzzy coat that can take three types, with a fairly straight style from the Cocker, a close curly coat from the Poodle, or an intermediate, wavy form that reflects a combination of the two, depending on whether it is derived more from one parent than the other.

Since the style of coat only becomes evident in pups over the age of six weeks, and all three forms may be found in one litter, prospective owners will want to wait until their puppy is selected after this stage. In several different coat colors, both strong and patterned, the "breed" arrives.

They include:

- Black
- White
- Cream
- Apricot
- Red
- Chocolate
- Silver
- Roan

Figure 1A cockapoo from US Breed

Some would exhibit both parents' physical features, and have a mildly

domed skull, an obvious pause, and a subtly tapering muzzle. In general, the eyes are brown in color, while merle dogs can have exceptionally light or blue eyes. In general, the ears are average in height, wedge-shaped, and while folded inward, sit upright at the base. The body shape is in proportion to the dog's size, being lean and strong, and not excessively broad.

Behavior and temperament:

A well-balanced Cockapoo is an irrepressibly cheerful and friendly dog who wants everyone he meets to be friends with. This has always been conceived as a companion breed, and it is affectionate and very devoted to its owners, willing to work hard to please them, like both of its parents. However, if breeders are not careful about their parent stock, it is important to be aware of the potential for nervousness in the Cocker Spaniel, which they can carry through, so these positive traits should never be taken for granted.

Happy, sociable dogs are the result of their upbringing rather than their genes, and the Cockapoo needs early, positive social experiences, like every dog. It is a good choice of dog for families, since it can quickly interact with more than one human, but it may be vulnerable to bullying from younger children.

CHAPTER TWO

House training:

The Cockapoo is a willing and able pupil because of its combination of intelligence and eagerness to please. Although herding breeds training will begin as early as eight weeks of age, socialization can take priority up to four months of age for the crucial time.

Potty training:

Supervision, consistency and repetition are the key to successful potty training. At times, you may get disappointed, as it can sometimes be one step forward and two back, but you will get there with perseverance and consistent training. Don't expect a puppy to learn overnight and they're all going to learn at various rates, so expect "accidents" to happen while learning and developing.

Make routine:

So, launch your routine preferably by having them out 1/2 an hour to the garden or field in which you want them to toilet hourly. After eating or drinking, waking up, and after a play session, before bedtime, toilet breaks should be considered, but daily periods are the secret to successful preparation.

At this time, don't play with them, or disturb them, since this is not playtime but bathroom time.

Without you, never let the puppy into the garden toilet and never leave the door open for him to come and go as they please until toilet training has been set up. Use a special term to show where you want them to go, then say something like "Go toilet" and heap plenty of praise and offer some treats when the puppy does. You should eventually minimize therapies, but as the dog is more educated, you can also compliment them.

Soon, he'll understand that the word is his cue to go. He can then have playtime after the toilet, so he can distinguish between the two in that way. If this procedure is replicated, you puppy will quickly learn what he needs to do, and he will realize that toileting means a bonus. Make sure they are in an environment where you don't mind "accidents" occurring at periods when you might not be able to track them. Or in a playpen or box.

Some signs to consider:

The common signs suggesting that the puppy needs to go to the toilet are that the puppy may begin to circle or sniff the ground, get agitated, whimper, and may go to the door for those who are into their routines. Though some do not show signs and just squat and go, but look carefully for the signs they will happen quickly and you will soon get to know which

When you see these signals, make sure you get the dog to their bathroom area soon, ensuring encouragement and reward when they go.

Rewarding positive behavior:

Upon good behavior of puppy, he should be awarded. This elaborates that when he shows a good or positive gesture in social environment, you should award him to encourage him for this behavior. This reward can be in terms of affection, love and providing his favorite food. This reward by you will develop a positive mindset of puppy. He will keep his positive behavior consistent and maintained.

You can reward him by playing a game with puppy. This will bring his attention to you and your family. In this way a puppy feels himself in a positive environment.

Crate training:

Why crate training:

The aim of your dog's crate training is to teach your dog to go on command for protection, obedience and general behavior management in its crate (a rectangular structure that serves as a replacement for a den). Dogs prefer cages, dogs prefer to go under desks, on sofas or on blankets the same way. The crate also offers a place for your dog where it is warm and secure.

Generally, dogs do not want their sleeping place to be soiled. A cage is also particularly successful in your dog's home exercise. Crate preparation is also beneficial for your pets while travelling with your pets, since a crate can be used to comfortably carry your pet dog. Overall, it is an efficient teaching technique that many dog owners and coaches alike have used effectively.

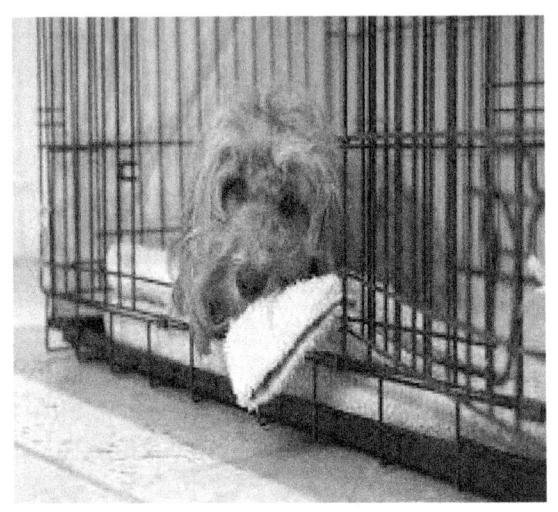

Choosing a crate:

The first thing to keep in mind is that to feel secure in it, the cockapoo crate needs to be huge enough for your cockapoo. Whenever he wants to, he has to be able to get up, sit down and turn around in it. And, if the cage is too small or not ventilated well enough, then this can be harmful for the welfare of the puppy. Certainly, the dog crate would help, but we suggest that you try out different sizes and find the best one for a little dog like your cockapoo.

Pick a crate and make sure it gives your

dog enough room, comfort and protection. To be able to stand up and walk about, the height of the crate should be big enough for your puppy. It should not be too big, though, otherwise it might use one corner as a toilet. Buying an adjustable cage that can fit him / her later as an adult dog is more reasonable and affordable if you have a puppy.

Cockapoo training for crate:

You'll want to keep things as fun and welcoming as possible if you're going to allow your dog to spend a lot of time in his crate. Putting one or two of his favorite toys inside it is one way to get started on this. Next, you'll want to throw in a towel or blanket that has its smell on it already.

Once he begins to show more interest in the crate, by throwing more treats in it, you can inspire him more. You obviously don't want to try to pull him in too easily or by shoving him in too physically, since this could throw him off the idea for good.

Start by playing around near the crate with your puppy. By putting favorite cookie or toy inside it, entice your dog into the crate. You might even feed dinner to your dog in the crate. Make sure to reward it more with encouragement and soft patting as the dog reaches the crate. This will aid with associating good thoughts for the crate. Repeat the method for the next few days until the crate is used and used without prompting.

What to do at night time:

Bringing the dog to sleep in here at night could be trickier than convincing him to get in during the day. If during the day you have tried to wear him out and wait till, he is exhausted before you bring him in, so there is a better likelihood that he can sleep easily and have a peaceful night.

To shut out the glare, some owners want to place a blanket over the crate, while others will place on soothing music for it. Then do your utmost to ignore him if he begins to whine or protest, as he can calm down quickly. When you take him out of his crate at night, it would be even harder in the long term to get him used to his crate.

For successful training:

Effective crate training for a dog is to equate it with the crate with all good stuff, even though it is alone in it. As a means of discipline for any misbehavior, never take a dog back to its crate. The relation between a dog and its crate must always be supportive.

CHAPTER THREE

Training in terms of exercise:

The Cockapoo is quite an amazing dog, and probably requires at least 30 to 60 minutes of regular exercise. The favorite method of exercise will vary, with some dogs maybe happiest when running off-lead, with their Cocker heritage more in tune, whilst others would want their humans as much as possible at their side. If offered the opportunity, they are athletic and enthusiastic enough to do well in professional sports.

Importance:

Originally bred to work for a hunter, the

Cocker spaniel is quite a utility dog.

Their responsibilities cover everything from long-distance running, water recovery, and game flushing. They are a hard worker who have a great deal of toughness. The Poodle is a very active breed as well and is very knowledgeable.

The Cockapoo has a lot of stamina as a result of being a combination of these two breeds, and wants regular walks and exercise. To keep them occupied, they are exceedingly affectionate and adore this type of activation.

They can be small to medium in size and being a blend would not always provide a Cocker Spaniel or a Poodle's energy levels, but they are normally fairly aggressive in most situations. They often need a good amount of emotional stimulus from the intellect they have received from the Poodle. One of the main causes of behavior disorders is frustration, so it helps to keep them amused.

There are 3 types of exercises for cockapoo:

1. Daily walk
2. Free play
3. Mental exercise

Types:

Daily walk:

For good pace, a cockapoo wants a regular walk of about 20-30 minutes at a good pace.

You will decide how long a walk they deserve by tracking your Cockapoo. When they pant heavily, lag behind, or stop and lie down, they're likely to have had enough. It is definitely a smart time to finish the walk. You can opt to walk a little faster while they are comfortably trotting along.

A quick daily stroll with a long walk at the weekend is more effective than none all week. You can take your Cockapoo on two shorter walks instead, if you like.

Obviously, even though they are the same breed, each dog is an individual.

Free-play and toys:

Toys:

Many toys are available in market to engage a puppy in activities. These are ideal for getting them to have fun and active play with your Cockapoo.

There are a number of dog toys that can be used for your dog to play alone. These are great for times when you don't have the time or you're otherwise occupied when your dog is home alone. This way, without your overt intervention, your dog will also receive both physical exercise and emotional relaxation.

Play with other dogs:

Give the Cockapoo the chance to play alongside other dogs. Not only is this perfect for consuming calories and relaxing their brains, but it also shows them essential social abilities.

Mental exercise:

From their daily walks and free play time, the Cockapoo gets some emotional relaxation and enrichment. However, the availability of other things that activate the mind is a smart idea. As much energy as physical activity, mental exercise will burn.

Some mental exercises for cockapoo are:

Learning:

To have mental enrichment, teaching new orders and tricks is also excellent. Teaching them the names of their toys is a common game that involves learning.

Hundreds of vocabulary and names can be acquired by dogs.

Enrichment of Food

Turn mealtimes into a chance for a mental workout and enrichment for your Cockapoo. Give them operations that enable them to labor for their calories, instead of feeding them from a dish.

Toys Puzzle

Puzzle toys are a perfect way to test the intellect of your dog and develop its problem-solving ability.

In summary:

So, how much exercise is needed for a Cockapoo? They are relatively healthy as a hybrid of the Cocker Spaniel and Poodle, have very high energy levels and love to play.

At least one stroll on a leash or off leash in the park for 30 minutes or more can be a regular workout. A great deal of free play and games and mental relaxation are expected in addition to the daily walk.

CHAPTER FOUR

Socializing the cockapoo:

For your puppy, everybody they meet, everything they see and everywhere they go will be a brand-new experience. And it is your job to make everything as pleasant as possible so that they understand to be comforted, confident and hospitable.

Introducing cockapoo with new people:

Once they get all their jabs, you won't be able to take your dog on walks, so you can introduce them to the car, traffic, the neighbors, the colleagues, the postman, and even buses and trains, if you can comfortably handle them. Let the puppy uscd to the noisy sounds inside the home, such as the washing machine, the phone and the vacuum cleaner.

You ought to behave calmly and cheerfully in all these circumstances. If the puppy gets stressed, don't push it, but give them plenty of encouragement and a little reward any time they respond well. Tip: ask individuals to offer their hands with palms up, or your puppy will perceive hostility friendliness.

If your dog hasn't seen any kids before, it might be a shock to them. Start by adding an older child and telling them not to squeal or make abrupt gestures if you can. They will soon learn to love children, but their playing should always be supervised by an adult.

Introducing with other puppies:

Take your puppy to visit the other dogs

for a short stroll. This can be overwhelming for both of you. Don't worry too much — adult dogs won't usually snap at puppies. Check with the other dog's owner, but normally it's better to leave your dogs to introduce themselves to one another. After a few seconds of sniffing, they normally play happily together. Again, the trust of your dog can be boosted by plenty of praise and tactical treats. A huge, jumping puppy, though, can fully overpower a smaller one, so it is typically safer to keep them apart until they are properly socialized.

Conclusion:

After having a puppy, the most critical factor is to train him using authentic means and techniques. A man usually thinks that after buying a cockapoo dog, he will be easily making him to adjust in the new environment. But in fact, the reality is opposite. The fact is that real challenges arouse after having puppy. Properly training a puppy to make him adapt the situation and adjusting in new environment is a real challenge. Now, the owner needs a comprehensive set of guidelines or instructions to cope with the challenge. This article is a complete set of those instructions to aware the owner about puppy training. The training techniques elaborating making a right place for puppy is explained. Training techniques of puppy have been discussed and analyzed in details. The training in terms of socialization to make puppy interact well with people and other dogs is also discussed in details. The physical and mental exercises along with their impact on health have been defined in details.

In short, all the details of puppy training

especially related to cockapoo has been discussed and elaborated in this article. This is a complete guide with comprehensive concepts of puppy training.

Printed in Great Britain
by Amazon